Action
Rhymes

Compiled by John Foster
Illustrated by Carol Thompson

Oxford University Press

Oxford   New York   Toronto

Oxford University Press, Great Clarendon Street, Oxford OX2 6DP

Oxford   New York
Athens Auckland Bangkok Bogota Bombay
Buenos Aires Calcutta Cape Town Dar es Salaam
Delhi Florence Hong Kong Istanbul Karachi
Kuala Lumpur Madras Madrid Melbourne
Mexico City Nairobi Paris Singapore
Taipei Tokyo Toronto

and associated companies in
Berlin   Ibadan

Oxford is a trade mark of Oxford University Press

This selection and arrangement © John Foster 1996
Illustrations © Carol Thompson 1996
First published 1996
Reprinted 1997

John Foster and Carol Thompson have asserted their moral
right to be identified as the authors of this work

A CIP catalogue record for this book is available
from the British Library

ISBN 0 19 276144 7

Printed in Belgium

Contents

Rocket

I am a rocket
crouched on the ground,
waiting quietly
without a sound.

Light this fuse
on my little toe . . .
Ready for take-off?
Here I go:
WOOOOOOOOOOSH!

Tony Mitton

Exercises

Bend your body,
touch your toes.

Straighten up,
and touch your nose.

Wave your arms,
now touch each knee.

Stamp your feet,
and count to three.
One, two, three!

Linda Hammond

See Me Walking

See me walking down the street,
Can you walk like me?
Walking with my head held high
As proud as can be.

See me skipping down the street,
Can you skip like this?
Throw your head back, look up high
And blow the sun a kiss.

See me jumping down the street,
Jumping oh so high.
Jump like me and stretch your arms
And try to touch the sky.

See me tip-toe down the street,
Softly on the ground.
Tip-toe tip-toe just like me,
Making not a sound.

See me hopping down the street,
Hoppety hoppety hop.
'Hop with me until we're tired
And then we'll have to stop.

Clive Webster

The Robot

I am a little robot,

I come from Outer Space!

My body's made of metal
and so's my head and face.

There's lots of wires inside me
and knobs and switches too,

so if you press this button
you'll see what I can do!

I start off very slowly, and then my arms begin to move
turn head from side to side, out straight and then spread wide.

My legs transport me forwards, together then apart.
Clank, clank, clank, clank, clank, clank, clank,

right back to the start!

Linda Hammond

That One's Me!

Have you seen a helicopter
hover in the sky?

Have you seen a jet
go screaming by?

Have you seen a submarine
glide beneath the sea?

Have you seen a bicycle?
That one's me!

Have you seen a frog
as it hops and leaps?

Have you seen a slug
as it slowly creeps?

Have you seen a squirrel
as it scampers up a tree?

Have you seen a roly-poly?
That one's me!

Tony Mitton

15

The Crop Song

This is the song the seed sings: sow, sow, sow.

This is the song the shoot sings: grow, grow, grow.

This is the song the root sings: deep, deep, deep.

And this is the song the farmer sings: reap, reap, reap.

Tony Mitton

When I Get Up in the Morning

When I get up in the morning
I tumble out of bed,
I yawn and stretch and stretch and yawn
And scratch my sleepy head.

When I get up in the morning
I always wash my face,
And splash and splash the soapy water
All around the place.

When I get up in the morning
I always clean my teeth,
Front and back and back and front,
On top and underneath.

When I get up in the morning
I always brush my hair,
Brush it this way, brush it that,
Brush it everywhere.

When I get up in the morning
I always rub my tummy,
Because I know my breakfast's waiting –
Yummy yummy yummy.

Clive Webster

When Susie's Eating Custard

When Susie's eating custard,
She gets it everywhere.
Down her bib, up her nose,
All over her high chair.

She pokes it with her fingers.
She spreads it on her hair.
When Susie's eating custard,
She gets it everywhere.

John Foster

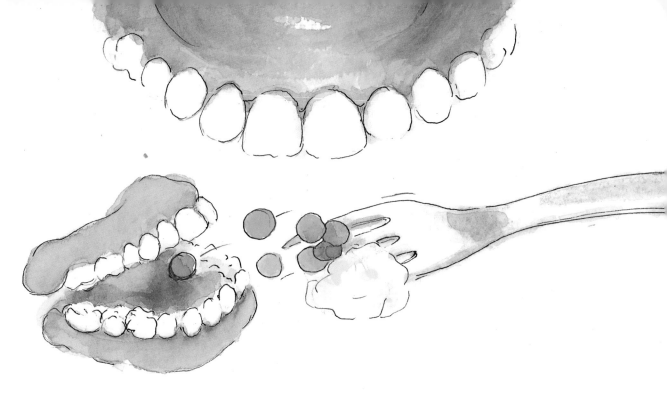

Teeth

Great big teeth,
Chomp, chomp, chomp, chomp,

Mashing up dinner,
Chomp, chomp, chomp.

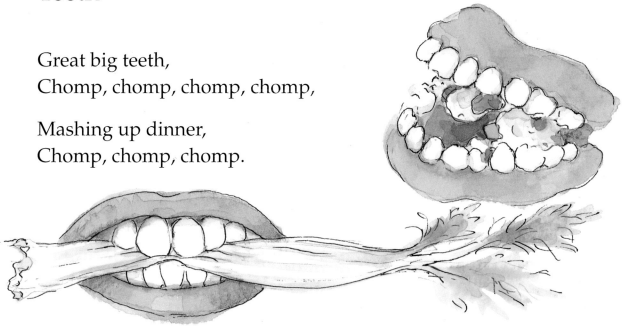

If we didn't give them so much work,
Chomp, chomp, chomp, chomp,

We'd all get thinner,
Chomp, chomp, chomp.

Wendy Cope

Walking Round the Zoo

Walking round the zoo,
What did I see?

An elephant that waved
Its trunk at me.

Walking round the zoo,
What did I see?

A parrot that squawked
And winked at me.

Walking round the zoo,
What did I see?

A crocodile that snapped
Its jaws at me.

Walking round the zoo,
What did I see?

A monkey that pointed
And laughed at me!

John Foster

23

Three Purple Elephants

There were three purple elephants,
A little pink mouse,
A black and white panda,
A yellow wooden house.

I opened the door
Of my yellow wooden house,
Said, 'Come inside, panda.
Come inside, mouse.'

The three purple elephants said,
'What about us?'
'I'm sorry but you'll have to get
The Number Five bus.'

Joan Poulson

Lazy Little Alligator

Lazy little alligator
lying in my lap,
let me sit and stroke you
as you take a little nap.

Hungry little alligator
waking in my lap,
wonders what's for breakfast:
SNAP! SNAP! SNAP!

Tony Mitton

Dinosaur Dreams

Dinah Shore dreamed she saw
a dinosaur
peeping round her bedroom door.

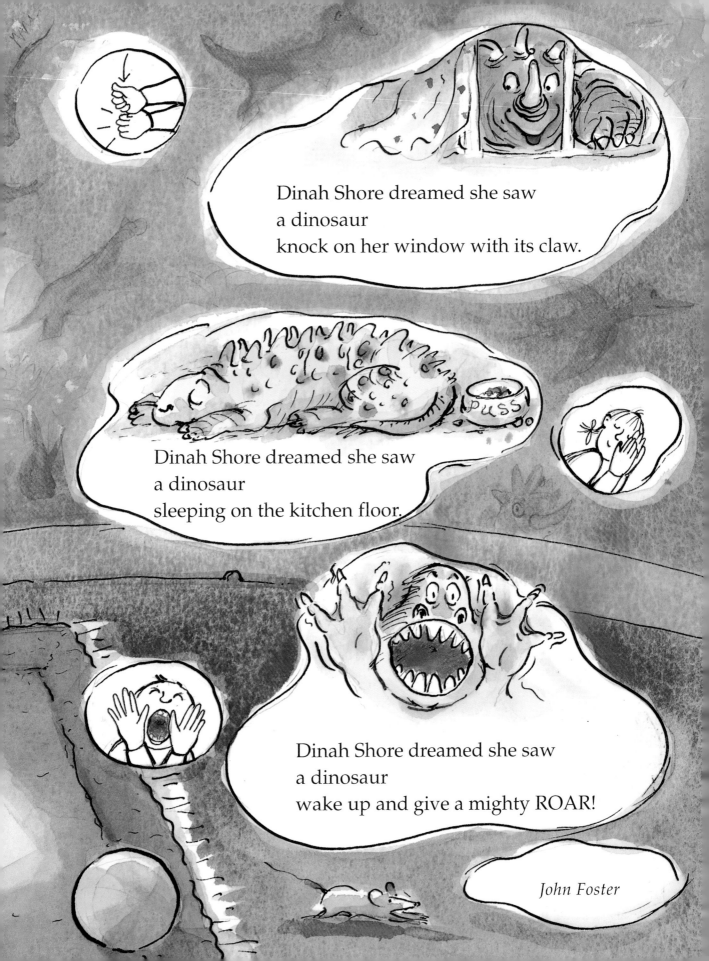

Dinah Shore dreamed she saw
a dinosaur
knock on her window with its claw.

Dinah Shore dreamed she saw
a dinosaur
sleeping on the kitchen floor.

Dinah Shore dreamed she saw
a dinosaur
wake up and give a mighty ROAR!

John Foster

Creepy Crawly Creatures

At night
before I go
to sleep,
the creepy, crawly,
creatures creep.
They creep into
my bed.
And then,
they tickle
my toes
and creep
out again.

Marie Brookes

We are grateful for permission to include the following poems in this collection:

Marie Brookes: 'Creepy Crawly Creatures', Copyright © Marie Brookes 1996, first published in this collection, by permission of the author. **Wendy Cope:** 'Teeth' from *Twiddling Your Thumbs: Hand Rhymes* by Wendy Cope, reprinted by permission of the publishers, Faber & Faber Ltd. **John Foster:** 'When Susie's Eating Custard', from *Food Poems* compiled by John Foster (OUP, 1993); 'Dinosaur Dreams' from *Dinosaur Poems* compiled by John Foster (OUP, 1993), both poems Copyright © John Foster 1993. 'Walking Round the Zoo' from *Themes for Early Years: Myself,* compiled by Irene Yates (Scholastic, 1995), Copyright © John Foster 1995. All poems reprinted by permission of the author. **Linda Hammond:** 'Exercises' from *One Blue Boat* by Linda Hammond (first published by Viking Children's Books Ltd, 1991), Copyright © Linda Hammond 1991, and 'The Robot' from *Five Furry Teddy Bears* by Linda Hammond (Puffin, 1990), Copyright © Linda Hammond 1990, reprinted by permission of Penguin Books Ltd. **Tony Mitton:** 'Rocket', 'That One's Me!', 'The Crop Song', and 'Lazy Little Alligator', Copyright © Tony Mitton 1996, first published in this collection by permission of the author. **Joan Poulson:** 'Three Purple Elephants', Copyright © Joan Poulson 1996, first published in this collection by permission of the author. **Clive Webster:** 'See Me Walking' and 'When I Get Up in the Morning', Copyright © Clive Webster 1996, first published in this collection by permission of the author.

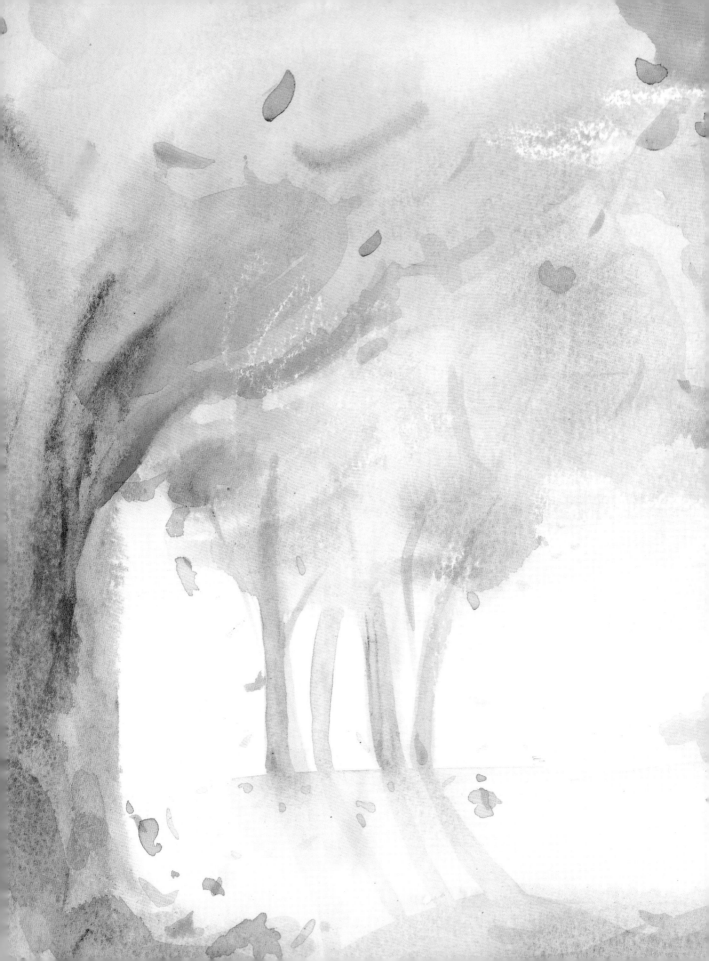